THE BOOK
WE
NEVER HAD

A GUIDE TO MENTAL FREEDOM

JACQUELINE FILENE TAYLOR POWELL

The Book We Never Had
A Guide to Mental Freedom

Paperback ISBN: 978-1-63812-094-0
Hardcover ISBN: 978-1-63812-096-4
Ebook ISBN: 978-1-63812-095-7

Published by Green Sage Agency   08/03/2021

Green Sage Agency
1-888-366-9989
inquiry@greensageagency.com

DEDICATION PAGE

*I am dedicating this book to my children, who
are my strength, pride, honor, and joy.
Erica Powell, Shanell Johnson,
Mia Knowles-Davis, and Darius Heslop.*

INTRODUCTION

We all go through things to grow. Growth through experience is a well-known phrase that we all look forward to. Growth? What is it, actually? I would say growth is understanding the why we go through things and knowing how to handle our emotions while going through experiences. We are all on a quest to purpose and life does not have to be as difficult as we make it. Do not get me wrong not every battle is easy, but when certain things are out of your control the only thing you can control is how you feel while going through your experience. I believe when we face the fact that experience and obstacles are indefinite it will allow us to embrace our trails. Life events happen and not always will life deliver to you what you want.

For a while I did not know how to provide a summary or descriptive detail regarding what my book was about. Until, one day I was being interviewed and I was asked, what did I want people to learn from this book.

Most self-help books are about the art of human nature. The knowing of self and life so that you can win. We are shaped and molded for our purpose on earth. I want people to understand that.

So many men, women, adults, and children have been through traumas, but we instinctively suppress those emotions. Suppressing emotions is something that individuals do automatically. Through my trails I have seen much victory as well as most people and I felt that there was no one that I could go to. No matter the amount of success or the amount of bills, everyone must experience something in life. I have learned that without struggle and pain there is no growth. How can you grow if everything is perfect? I searched for something or someone to explain life as raw as possible, because there is no sugar-coating hardship. I could not find someone to explain nor prepare a manual on how to handle the fact that life will bring you discomfort. Even though each trauma is not the same it all affects us equivalently. There are ways to handle our circumstances.

There are ways to analyze and to accept the privations we experience.

There was no book out here that was as blunt to the needs of adversity. No one talks about the mental battles that we grow through collectively. It is as if these things are ignored. Nor does anyone analyze the experiences that may have structured certain morals in life. This is the book we never had. A guide to mental freedom.

CHAPTER 1

NOTHING YOU HAVE BEEN THROUGH SHALL BE WASTED...

What is Purpose?

Everyone has their own definition as to what purpose is. Purpose for all of us is different because of our personal perspectives. No one gets to not go through challenges. Change comes from challenges and we must learn to welcome the challenge for the change. A lot of us do not think the same because of the things we have experienced. There is purpose within experience because the things we have been through shapes and molds the way we interpret life. Life lessons gives us the ability to gain common sense and logic for our journey.

Purpose to me is identifying your inner person and your inner gifts. Your purpose is to identify what your gifts are. To understand why you are here is purposeful. There is power in growth and strength in understanding. I like to define purpose as working on your inner self and being true with who you are throughout your experience on this earth. Our purpose is to search and explore those things that define meaning because you are never done learning. There is always something to acknowledge and learn. I do not feel that self-purpose is something that is associated with anyone else. Your purpose is your purpose. You were created for your own purpose in life. That is why we cannot blame others for what we do or go through because one thing that you own is your purpose.

A lot of people have misconstrued the meaning of purpose. People think that purpose is subject to fame. Everyone has a purpose, and it does not have to be luxury. It can be something simple. We are connected to the universe. We are connected to purpose to fulfill a task. It is our responsibility to figure out that thing that solves purpose. We spend all our lives searching for something that we are supposed to be doing because we constantly feel that we are not doing enough. Nine times out of ten we are doing exactly what it is that we are meant to be doing.

Most of us become frustrated with what we feel is not enough. A lot of people would be happy if they accept their purpose. People get so caught up in the standards of basic living. Go to school they say, become rich and famous they say. Most individuals are focused on the wrong things in life. Most people feel like if they are not famous than they are not fulfilling their purpose in life. Purpose is life's fulfillment. Everything and everyone have a purpose.

We all have a different purpose and I think that people get it confused. I have heard people say that everyone on earth shares the same purpose. If there were true THEN everyone would think the same for the same purpose to be fulfilled. If we lived in a world with everyone fulfilling the same purpose than there would be no reason for leaders. Everyone would share the same experience.

Everyone has a purpose and for everyone purpose is different. That is why it is important to know your purpose because when you do not know you get caught up in what everyone else around you are doing. You start to witness what works for the next person and automatically think that it is supposed to work for you. Your purpose is what you give. It is the gift you use to give. What do you give to the world?

The Purpose of Experience

The things that we go through, we go through for a reason. Our experiences are a part of our purpose. Whatever you give is an experience and you must give the experience that you want. A lot of experiences are not good, but you learn something. Experiences enhance your purpose. Some people may think that winning the lottery is a great experience, but what you do with your experience defines purpose. For an example, the person that has been abused can either have their experience define them or they can define it. Your experience can either build you or break you. It is your choice.

People may abuse your body or try to abuse you mentally, but no one can break your spirit. Your spirit is something that you control. You cannot give power to your experience.

The greatest thing about experience is that it empowers you if you learn from it. You should use bad experiences to empower yourself and not beat on yourself. Do not allow bad experiences to weaken you but empower you. Experience is there to make you stronger within your purpose. You must embrace the things that you go through so that you can understand what the purpose of it is for. You must take your bad experiences and think to yourself on how it may empower you. Every experience you must take as a lesson. We must learn to not take experiences so personal. Nothing is really meant to hurt us yet strengthen us.

Yes. Some people do go through deeper pain, but there is a greater strength on the other side of pain. If you are negative with your experience you will eventually mourn your experience. Your mind will tell you that is who you are, and you will begin to define your worth as a person from those negative thoughts. Embrace bad things and learn from them. If you focus on the bad things of your experience you will not be able to focus on the glory of the experience.

Everything Has Purpose

Everything has purpose and some of us fear the why. That is why we panic and get frustrated with life. We do not have a blueprint as to who, what, where, why, and when. God created everything with purpose, and you must find that purpose. We are all explorers on the universe. You can never give up. Where there is a will there is a way. If you do what you are supposed to do in life, you will eventually find your purpose. You should also learn how not to sweat the small things.

It is imperative to understand that you must go with the flow. Laughing is important you must realize that you cannot control everything. The things that have purpose will happen. It is not up to us to control it. We must be mindful of the experience and take whatever lessons that come with it.

Take Wisdom from Every Experience

We are always in training for the next experience. Life does not just stop at one obstacle. There is always something to go through. Life is about growing and what is life without the growing pains.

There are few things that you can take from experience. Because I would like to think about it this way, you should only have to go through something one time but sometimes God will allow you to go through things twice. If you do not get it correct the first time sometimes seeking victory through a second chance is more beneficial. There is always something God wants us to learn when we go through things. Sometimes it can be as common as to share wisdom with the next person so that they would not have to go through it. I like to say that wisdom is greater than knowledge because wisdom is understanding, and knowledge is knowing. It is easy to know what you are going through but once you gather the understanding of your experience you have gathered a part of wisdom. Wisdom is something that we take with us throughout our experience on earth. Most experience leads to victory. As most old school folks would say, "anything that does not break you, makes you stronger." Some people allow their circumstance to get the best of them. You cannot allow temporary situations to affect you for a lifetime. I have seen people destroy themselves over one situation. There are many things that makes a person want to break, but once you get in your head that you are bigger than your situation you then allow the understanding of your process to present itself. You will then understand that nothing you have been through shall be wasted.

Nothing You Have Been Through Shall Be Wasted

I am a very strong woman and I know that because I know what I was able to persevere through. I do not have regrets. I do not walk around with them because then I cannot keep my spirit the way I want to. Nothing that ever happened to me was a regret, it was an experience.

Nothing we have been through is for vain. Everything has its place in life. Even though we do not know the plan of God and what he has in store for the universe, we can acknowledge that it is for a reason. So, nothing we have been through is wasted; we do not know what God is using it for.

What I have learned from experience

Experience has taught me to think fast. There is never a block in my mind because I am also strategizing on what has the potential to be next. Experience has taught me to always have a plan as well as an option that follows. I do this so that I will not be disappointed. I have learned that experience is temporary and depending on the person it may have a lifetime effect. I like to look at experience as a training process because each experience prepares you for the next obstacle. People sit and plan their life, but people never think what life may have planned for them. Whatever life chooses to throw your way, you must adapt. I have also learned that it is important to understand what you are going through. Experience is not the problem it is what you do with your experience that may help or hinder you while on your journey. Life is hard and you must be prepared. You must tell yourself; this is what happened, and this is what I need to do.

Embracing your challenges in life is not something that happens over night, but it is a choice. You can choose to have you, and everyone else around you feel sorry for your choices or you can make others wish they were handling situations as yourself. You must do the best you can in life. The only person that can make the best decision for you is you.

Understanding what you are going through is important.

It is important to be able to discern what you are going through so that you know how to make decisions for your experience. If you do not understand what you are going through it can affect your next decision, which impacts your decisions moving forward. You can have a clue where you are headed in life just from the experiences that you have encountered. If you do not understand what you are going through from where you are than if the situation presents itself again you will do the same thing expecting a different result. That is insanity.

CHAPTER 2

I AM IN TRAINING...

It Never Ends There

As I stated previously. There is always something to go through. Some of the things we go through are easier to deal with than others. Being that there are so many things to go through the formalities of growth are learned during obstacles. We are always in training. To elaborate in a fonder sense; with training there is always a life lesson to learn. There will always be wisdom to gain. You must train your mind and your body because there is always a battle to preserve through.

The things we encounter affects us spiritually and physically and we must know how to gain our strengths through experience. Life has enough influence to affect everything about us. Everyday there is a different familiarity to gain concept for. There is always a lesson that we are learning or training for. There are a lot of things we are in training for but there is usually one thing that settles in our spirit. Oprah likes to call it an "Aha moment." Some people may call it a gem. Whatever it is, it was meant for you to grasp sense of the lesson. Our lessons are endless, so it is important that we understand the cards we are dealt.

Battle Entry and Second Chances

You can sense when something is about to happen and for some people you cannot sense it at all. My kids used to say that I sleep too much. Some people might say they want to lose weight, but then they smoke because most people replace a habit with another one. There is always something else to enter. Circumstances are often present, but the lesson allows us to be adequate for what is next. it is a battle, a mental battle as well as an emotional and physical battle. The list goes on. It reminds me of a scenario that I usually express to people to comprehend the analogy.

Imagine that there are a million bandages on you. You do not know which bandage may fall off or which scar you will have to heal. Each scar represents something that you have already been through and no one likes to repeat a tribulation, but sometimes we must gather the gem needed. Each wound is preparation for the next. Once a band aid falls off you recognize what that pain feels like and you know how to heal from it because you have been through it before. That is why it is imperative that we understand our trials.

We cannot get frustrated when we go through something more than once. Obviously, it is something that you have not focused on that you need to learn.

There is nothing wrong with second chances. Commonly it is a blessing sensing victory twice. Just as we are in training its often grace that the trainer is allowing you a do over. When I say trainer; it is a title for whomever your higher power is. So, if you must retake a test you go back in understanding what you have been through before.

It is a learning experience. Sometimes experiences are not battle's, being good, nor bad, but it is a learning experience to prepare you for a tribulation. While you are in training and you want to pass the first test but a lot of the times when you pass it the first time you did not learn anything. Only because most of us think we know it all and we go into everything knowing that we will be victorious and not knowing that there is also something to learn. Being optimistic is not the problem, but arrogance will prove you wrong each time.

While going through an obstacle for the second time we are reminded of what we learned during the repeated situation. Being that it happened before you must ask yourself did you learn anything to enhance self, or did you allow your situation to make you weak. Because if your situation made you weak it is going to come around again, but this time it is going to see if you can take it or if it is going to take you. Most of the time we do not realize the reason our battles must double back. Typically, it is because we have not learned anything the first time. Being that our experiences shape and mold us we continue to be pressed by experiences until we are diamond cut. It is like when you are driving and you have been somewhere before, but you go at it again, but this time you make a different turn. Some people say, oh I got lost. You did not get lost. You just went into a different direction. You learned a new way. You cannot learn lost. You can only learn a new way. There are lessons in life that is going to circle back and once you realize that you become more relaxed within your process.

A lot of us need to learn patience. Most of the time we do not understand the reason we have to double back with our experiences. Usually, it is because there was something that we did not learn the first time. There is never one way to get somewhere. Sometimes it may be three or four ways. You just so happened to turn down the way that you chose. It does not make you right or wrong. It means that you are learning.

You are learning through your battles.

I tell many young women that I come across that life is about learning. The more you understand that life is not against you and only trying to teach you that is when you accept evolvement of self. When change presents itself, it may come with a challenge. We can either accept the challenge or be defeated because challenges are going to happen. God has never promised us when, how, or where. He only promised us purpose and that is why we have life.

No one on this earth is secluded from circumstances. We all go through battles. When you understand the things, you go through it makes your path smoother. You must learn what worked or is working for you so that you will know how to maneuver while on your path. While on your path the number one thing is that you must find the inner joy that is embedded within you. You must also learn to lose your fear. When you are in training once you have let go of freedom, you are free.

Through battles you gather just enough information to get through it. Some people do not learn what was needed because things often move fast.

Or they think they know it all, so they were not able to learn what was needed. We can often be distracted by our own confidence. Even though you may have finished your battle, but now you must go deal with it. When you must deal with it you second guess yourself.

You second guess yourself when you are in training because you want to do it right the first time because that's how people perceive things. Our parents usually tell us to do it right the first time so that we do not have to it again. There is nothing wrong with going through the same test. It is like reprogramming yourself and refreshing yourself as needed.

You cannot negate your experiences.

There is always something to go through and again; once us as humans understand this, life becomes much easier. No matter who you are, you cannot ignore the fact that at times life will get hard. It is going to get rough. Life can be exceptionally challenging, and the pressures of this world can leave many people suicidal. Most of us have been to that point where we would like to end it all, permanently.

A lot of people become suicidal due to the pressures of life. Sometimes life can be overwhelming, but we must understand that most things can be fixed, but you cannot get back life. Death cannot be fixed. You must give yourself a chance because there is always some type of help that you can get. Even though I do understand those who made the decision to end it. I am not throwing them under the bus, but you cheat yourself when you commit suicide.

When you get to that point of facing the end you must get help. There will always be something that may get you back to that moment of ending it all and you must know how to deal with it. I have noticed that when people get to that point of pressure it is typically because they cannot handle change or things not changing. Most rich people cannot handle being broke and most poor people want to be rich. A lot of people fear their circumstances and that is where most people fold under pressure.

We must learn how to live within our circumstances as well as becoming carefree of the thoughts of others. I have come across a lot of people who base their life and live their life for the liking of others around them. It breaks my heart to see people not wanting to be themselves. We are all uniquely created, and it takes self to realize self-importance. You must have a nonchalant attitude about what others think. You cannot conform self to the acceptance of others. Stay in your lane and live for you.

You are not depressed, you are regrouping.

There is always some sort of help that you can get when you feel the need to regroup. Most people like to say that people are depressed. I have recently learned that there are many levels to depression. I do not say that I am depressed. I stopped using the word depressed a long time ago.

People like to use the word depressed to make you feel like something is wrong with you. I tell people that I am regrouping. You cannot allow this world to place labels on you. I say that I am regrouping because that is what it is. Regrouping for me means that there are some things that are going on with me that do not make me feel normal. Depression is a word that makes people feel like there is something wrong with them. There is nothing wrong with you, you are simply regrouping. It is okay to regroup and take time for self. Regrouping makes you stronger. It is important that you remain positive while regrouping.

I often tell people when they get to that space where they do not feel like their self it only means that it is time to regroup. When you are constantly dealing with other people daily or if you have suffered a major lost. It is important to take time for self to gather yourself. Regrouping is you finding yourself. It is you understanding that you need to take time for yourself. Often you must retrain your faith and that happens while regrouping. You cannot get stuck in an obstacle because everything is a process. You must trust your own process and never dwell on the small things.

Everything has an outcome, and you control if that outcome is a positive or negative. You have power and I speak that upon everyone reading this.

Survival Skills While in Training

First, you must always keep God in the forefront. I have persevered through many things due to prayer. You must have a relationship with God. He is your couch while in training and he will direct your path. You must keep your faith because it will help guide you, as well as assure you that you will be okay. I must keep my faith because if something is going on with me, God already knows about it. I must be alert when he sends clarity to me.

Second, you must learn how to have patience. Patience is extremely important. While going through life you can make it worst by moving too fast. You must trust your process. If you believe that you have a purpose in life and you have faith, then having patience is a given. It is a hard skill to learn because when you do not know your purpose or unsure of it, it makes it hard to have patience. With patience you will eventually know your purpose. You cannot move too fast and try to create your own purpose.

The third thing is that you must do other people right. Learn to be a blessing to others so that God can be a blessing to you. Be thankful for the things that you want to be thankful for.

Learning the basics

While in training you must be open minded because what you feel and perceive comes from someone else. As kids we are told what to do and how to do it by our parents. As citizens we obey the law of the land. We have conformed ourselves to someone else's rules. The reason we make certain choices in life comes from what we were taught from someone else and they have gathered what they were taught from someone. So, it is a chain reaction of lessons. So, while you are in training you must be open minded. You must have your mind made up. Your mind is powerful.

Individuals should learn what makes sense to self. So, it is a battle to not carry on what you were taught but enhance your lessons with what you know and what you feel. It is not bad that people share their experiences, but it becomes a problem when we base our experiences and lessons to someone else's lessons.

If it is not in your guide for what you are supposed to do, you are going to have a conflict and that is the point where people get confused and the frustration begins. People often get confused only because you are in training and what you learn from a child into a grown adult is just a basic guide. As you get older you will adapt different things and all you will need to do is enhance the basic things with your self-knowledge. Often people do not add the basics that their parents have taught them. If we can enhance from birth of what we learned, we can enhance our basics.

The "basics" are lessons. It is lessons that we learn. It is the general common sense that has been given to us by our parents. I say enhance your basics because they are generational lessons. Your parents learned from their parents and even though they are lessons passed down; you must enhance your basics because the world is not like that anymore. Parents often get frustrated and say things like, "Didn't I tell you to do it this way." The world is not like how it used to be. That is why you should only use the basics when needed. As a mother it was hard for myself because I was raised in a world that said you must teach your kids this and they should grow up and to be this or that. As parents we often push our kids to what we want them to be based on our own mistakes in life. Instead, we must allow our kids the intellectual freedom to gather a sense of life on their own. I give my kids the opportunity to be their self and to trust their own best interest.

You cannot be afraid of your own best interest. It is your power and never give that power or give someone control over you to even have the say so, over your best interest. When you lose your power, you get angry and you become disappointed. So, while in training I feel like your emotions and the basic things that you have learned should be intertwined which you see as person. the basic is fine because it gives you something to start with like the end resolution should be what you decide in which you feel or do not feel. If you give your power of best interest away, you give away your responsibility to freedom. When you have control over your own will power you have more strength. As individuals we must utilize our own will power and judgement. No one on earth can live your life for you. You must use your own mind and your own feelings. You cannot use the basics of what your parents taught you. I do not care who the parents are. The most powerful thing that was given to us is having a mind of our own. We are all humans, but we are all purposeful. To understand what your destiny will be on this earth you have to structure yourself to enhance your basics. If you do not do it, you will be lost. We have different roles in life and different purposes. It is imperative that you understand what you are going through for your own future and current experiences.

Life is an assignment and if you are alive there will always be something to learn. If you are alive you have an assignment.

CHAPTER 3

LIFE IS AN ASSIGNMENT.

Life is an assignment.

If you google what the definition of assignment is, you will find that it is a noun. A person, place, or thing. It means to be assigned a task or a piece of work as a part of a job or course study. When I say that life is an assignment it means that you are ready to fulfill a purposeful task. First, you have an assignment, then you gather your experience which fulfills your purpose.

When people say things like, there is always something or if it is not one thing then it is another. That means that there is always an assignment to complete. There is always something to do. If you are alive you will indefinitely be on an assignment. To do an assignment, you must do research. It is like being in school, once your teacher gives you a task that is now your assignment. You must find information to gather to complete your task. Typically to fulfill your task in life you research the things that you have already been through to complete your mission.

A lot of people do not know what their assignment is. A lot of people confuse their assignment with their purpose. It is like playing games.

You must complete certain challenges to get to the next level. Once you have completed all the levels you have completed your purpose. The game is life. The Levels are the assignments and the challenges within the level are your experiences. Just like a game, God will equip you for your assignment. I remember the James Bond game and during certain challenges you will find the get-well kits and whatever gun you needed for your mission. It is the same with God and your own assignments.

Most people lack to pay attention to the details in life to figure out what they are or have experienced. The things that you go through is a part of your assignment. I tell people that I do not feel the need to put up curtains because I never feel like that is where I am going to end.

Your assignment is your journey, and we travel from experience to experience. Your assignment is going to make you travel and do things. Your assignment will make you grow. It is your way and your life. Having your kids is an assignment. The way you teach and nurture your kids is an assignment because you are preparing them for their duty. There is always a mission that God has for you.

Once your assignments have been completed that means that your calling has been completed. You must associate your life to an aim. Once I have completed one assignment, I always ask God, what is next? You must allow your assignment to take you where you need to go and have faith while you are on your journey. The main weapon that people forget to equip themselves with is Faith. Faith will bring everything together. I have seen miracles happen just by trusting God while understanding that I am a willing vessel. You must have enough faith to carry you on. When you have an assignment, everything works for what you are supposed to do. You will not fail. I live off my assignment and my timeframe. I no longer question my assignment. I just do it.

People leave footprints.

You are never alone. Every life we encounter someone leaves their footprints on our path. Relationships are purposeful as well.

There is a very popular saying, people come in your life for a reason, a season, and some forever. Relationships and friendships are assignments. Often, we come across people that need our help or we need their help. I am the type of person that people confide into. Words have an assignment. Our words work for us so what you may say to someone that has crossed your path could have been your assignment. Words are influential and they travel with purpose and intention. You can talk to someone on a bus that you do not know, and it could be the little conversation that may have influence that individual to do something that they needed to do. Your words could have given that person strength. When you involve people into your life you have to ask your, why are they here. It is for you or it can be for them.

When people come into your life you must understand that not everyone is your soulmate. You must understand that every smiling face you come across is not your friend.

You must understand the objective of people that cross your path. Not everybody is going to do what you do. You must respect the differences of others. We were all uniquely created.

No one must conform to your expectations as a person. It takes the individuality away from a person. Somebody is going to teach you something and you are going to teach somebody something. Some people are toxic and that is why you must be strong, because everyone has an assignment. Even the trees outside. They are meant to grow. The rain has an assignment. Everybody and everything have an assignment.

If you are on this earth you are supposed to be doing something. Everyone is here for some reason and purpose. You must be able to acknowledge the things you are good at and may not be good at. You must recognize your own strengths and weaknesses.

It could be that someone has been through something and they are hurting, and they need you to heal them. You must pass on good aura while crossing paths with other people. You must love and embrace with love while crossing the path of others. Even the devil has an assignment, and his assignment is to steal, kill, and destroy. A lot of people say I am upset that the devil because he did this or that, the devil had an assignment. Your assignment is to be strong and to obtain the strength that God gave you. You must remind yourself that you live in this world, but you are not of this world. You have an assignment.

When you meet people, you cannot prejudge them because you do not know if they are a part of your assignment. Each encounter has something to do with your own mission, even if it was for you or the other person.

The Assignment for Family.

It is interesting how God has structured our families as one. You have your Aunties, Grandma, cousins, Parents, and siblings for a reason. Your family are your loved ones for a reason.

There is purpose with the connections we have with people on this earth, whether it is family, friends, the Wal-Mart clerk, etc. You must be mindful of your experience with people that cross your path. Family is the most important because like everyone says, no one can hurt you worse than family. You are connected to a specific bloodline for a reason and you must understand your ancestral goal.

I am my kid's mothers for a reason. There is no other parent or parents that could have equipped my kids better than me. I even made the best mistakes because even my mishaps made them better.

The Father and Mother

The father and mother are the most important factors. As a woman no matter who the Father is you nominated that man to be the Father of your child. I wanted to address that because I see a lot of females very upset at a man, they said yes to. I also see men upset at the woman they chose. Regardless of the Man or Woman, you created an offspring with the person you chose. For the sake of child, you must forget about all toxicity. Parents that hate each other do not oppose enough strength to set aside internal emotions for the betterment of the child. It is all fun and games until a child is born. Both parents have a responsibility, but you cannot force someone to do something they do not want to do. I tell mothers that hate the man they choose to look in the mirror because it reflects self.

As the mother you must ask yourself what you were going through to select a man that you deem to be a horrible person. So, when you tell your kids that that their mother or father is this and that, you are talking about yourself. It does nothing but let the child know that you were not functional at the time to see the things that you now see in their Father. This situation is one of the biggest problems I have learned.

Accept NOT Knowing

In conclusion of your purpose, being in training, and your life being an assignment. You must accept not knowing. Accept that sometimes you may not know every answer and you may have to go with the flow. Accept that God brought you here on earth for a reason. Even if you do not know Gods end game, accept not knowing.

We are not meant to know every little thing. That is why there is a such thing of mystery.

If we had the answer to everything we would not need to go on a journey or quest. There would be no reason for motivation or strength. I want everyone to know that you have a purpose. Each experience is a test to gather information because you are in training. Life is an assignment, and you are here for a reason. If you understand this and take those three jewels with you in life, you will then understand that, yes you have feelings, but you cannot have your emotions to control your circumstances because everything is temporary. Life gets hard for everyone. God is not just picking on you. We are all trying to become something greater with the hand that was dealt to us. You will be better. You are better. Be better because this is now the book you will always have.

If you are contemplating hurting yourself and/or know of someone, please contact, National Suicide Prevention Lifeline at 800-273-8255.

ACKNOWLEDGEMENTS

I would like to take the time to thank my son-in-law Duran Reeves and my daughter-in-law Asha-Lee Facey-Johnson for being a part of my family and making sure I never have to cook again, because of all the wonderful meals they prepare. To my bff and more Monica Chamberliss, you mean the world to me, Thelma and Louise forever! Major thanks also to my special counselor Johna Yashenko, who keeps me straight each week. Thanks for guiding me for years. You are truly a God sent. I appreciate you all.